Magical THINKING

Winner of the 2001
Ohio State University
Press / The Journal
Award in Poetry

Joseph Duemer

Magical THINKING

POEMS

THE OHIO STATE UNIVERSITY PRESS

Columbus

Library of Congress Cataloging-in-Publication Data
Duemer, Joseph
    Magical thinking : poems / Joseph Duemer.
        p. cm.
    ISBN 0-8142-0889-4 (alk. paper)—ISBN 0-8142-5087-4 (pbk. : alk. paper)
    I. Title

PS3554.U3145 M34 2001
811'.54—dc21

                                                                2001036634

Text and jacket design by Diane Gleba Hall.
Type set in Galliard by Sans Serif.
Printed by Thomson-Shore.

    9   8   7   6   5   4   3   2   1

ACKNOWLEDGMENTS

Some of the poems collected here have appeared previously in literary journals, often in different versions. I am grateful to the editors of the following publications for permission to reprint poems that originally appeared in them: *American Literary Review, American Poetry Review, Ascent, Blue Moon Review, Cửa Sổ Văn Hóa Việt Nam* [*Vietnam Cultural Window*] (Viet Nam), *Field, 5 AM, Georgia Review, Laurel Review, Red Rock Review, Salt* (Australia), *Salt Creek, Salt Hill Journal, Stand* (UK), and *Tampa Review.*

"The Best Meals of My Life" is included in *Spud Songs,* an anthology published by Helicon 9 Editions to benefit anti-hunger organizations; "Superstition" and "Theory of Tragedy" were included in my previous collection *Static,* published by Owl Creek Press in 1996, but are reprinted here out of thematic necessity. "For Wittgenstein" and "Wildlife of the Desert" were included in the chapbook *Primitive Alphabets,* published by White Heron Press in 1997. "For Wittgenstein" was commissioned by David Rakowski and is included in the song cycle for soprano *Silently, A Wind Goes Over,* published by Edition Peters (score no. 67616).

I am grateful to Clarkson University and the United States Information Agency for grants that allowed me to travel to Viet Nam in 1997 and 1999, respectively—this book would not exist without their generous support. And in my craft and sullen art I have been lucky in my friends—thanks to John Allman, John Balaban, Wendy Carlisle, H. L. Hix, Ly Lan, John Serio, Vang Anh, Candice Ward, and Mark Weiss for their criticism and love.

"For Wittgenstein" is for David Rakowski, who asked for it. "The Fall of Saigon" commemorates a brief meeting with Nguyen Ngoc Thanh Thuy (HCMC, summer 1997), and "Talking to Ghosts" is for Ronald Johnson, my teacher in 1972. "Youthful Journals" is for Carole Mathey—in Vietnamese, the words for *my house* are the same as the informal words for *spouse*: we have built our house. "Wildlife of the Desert" is for Michael Gessner, who appears to have walked into the desert himself.

FOR CAROLE

O God! I could be bounded in a nutshell

and count myself a king of infinite

space, were it not that I have bad dreams.

—Hamlet II.ii

CONTENTS

3.

I.

Đì ra một ngày, về một sàng khôn.

Go out one day, come back with a basket full of knowledge.

—Vietnamese proverb

MAGICAL THINKING: VIETNAM

Who can say for sure what
connects to what—parts
of a sentence or pieces
of a dream almost recalled.
Everything is a conductor
when the voltage is high enough—
air itself a plasma, an arm
of light made of free electrons
reaching out from a cloud
to bury its fist in the moist earth.
It can knock you down so you
won't get up, static obliterating
the song your nerves sing.
There are butterflies I see
only in the fall, black with gold-
edged wings, about the size
of a birch leaf folded in half—
mourningcloaks they're called,
& if you look closely just inside
the fringed edge of the wings
when they stand still on a stalk
of grass there are gas-jets of flame
that stand for grief. This reads
too much like a story, I know,
but last summer I saw them
in Viet Nam, an arcing cursive
signature above some graves.
Tell me there is no connection.
When I was in high school—
& this too must sound like fiction—
& my father still had a chance
at something like respect,
he hated poetry & threw away
the books I brought home,
snatching one from my hands
as if it were on fire while

behind us in the family room
the television chuckled.
It was clear he wanted me to go
to Vietnam—clear he already
thought of me as dead.

An educated man, Ngô Đình Diệm
believed in the power of words
to make a difference in the world
of things. So in a poetic gesture

he renamed the dangerous provinces
west of his capital, calling them
Hứa Nghĩa," a literary cliché that means
deepening righteousness. He called

the district center Khiêm Cường,
modest but vigorous, replacing
the old name Bầu Trại, *round farm*.
In the summer of 1963 the word was

becoming flesh. The president meant
to deceive the spirits of the air & earth
who had lived long in that place,
but they were not fooled, even by poetry.

POEM ON HIS BIRTHDAY

In the present world poetry
must be in love with science.
Recent studies confirm that
my life has swerved sideways—
As a child I felt the soft mist
falling when the crop dusters
overshot the cotton field that
bordered the river, organic
molecules settling on my tongue
& into the clear pools of my eyes
as I backstroked languidly
the warm green water. Slow
but muscular catfish patrolled
the bottom muck, their eyes
beads of mercury oxide: to these
I owe my jumpy disposition
& confusion over long division.
To say nothing at all of the
Maxwell-Boltzmann equations
that even before relativity
& the uncertainty principle
& the paradoxical results
of quantum calculations are said
to govern the fate of my cells,
themselves marvelous little sacs
of chemistry. I offer this prayer
over the passive voice of authority:
I accept that I am the sum miracle
of accidents in microcosm
& macrocosm. So: let me rock & roll
in this the temple of my body
as long as it lasts, a construction
of rhythm & blues & the righteous
anger of old Amos, who was
a natural-born man lovingly
unfolding the ten dimensions

of rage for his neighbors. I will
be happy from now on, please
God, may my language break so
cleanly out of my body.

THE BEST MEALS OF MY LIFE

When I crack an egg
I usually think
of the French girl
who lived downstairs
in the boarding house
where I endured
the winter following
my first marriage.
She would never
go to bed with me
but showed me instead
in her generosity
how to slip my finger
in a circle inside
the two halves of
a freshly broken
eggshell to extract
the last slick white
to dribble it into
the skillet. Her parents
had lived through
Nazi poverty & she
lectured me—profligate
& depraved—on thrift
& virtue. Out of kindness
she gave me instead
of what I wanted
meals of potatoes
& eggs & that is
the way, isn't it, of virtue—
to give not pleasure
but what is necessary
to sustain life: eggs
& potatoes & salt,
over which it becomes

possible to talk
& even to think.
Life of the body,
life of the mind.

ANARCHY OF DESIRES

Memory is among the functions of poetry.
I remember the fine summer night
we walked from the Blue Moon back
to my place long past midnight—miles
through the city, high clouds lit by neon
& streetlights bending our shadows.
We knew then though we couldn't have
said it we would be married the next year.
Our sexual concentration sharpened
our senses into an intoxication that filled
the precincts of the solar system.
It doesn't matter that later everything
went wrong in our lives—a sadness so
deep it stops the mind & shrivels the heart.
I want to remember in a lyric the night
we walked through the city on our way
to marriage though I no longer believe
in the lyric: we were drunk & drunk
on each other (though sober by the time
we were through with each other),
delighted with our muscles & the ways
skin moved over bone. We were tired
when we arrived but talked & talked,
tuned to the music of pure nakedness.
There was astonishment in everything
& though an incommensurate event
would occur between us & I am married
to a life on the far side of the continent,
I send to you & it is no lie my love
& my love for everything that once
we were, full of belief in our capacities.
We threw parties people still remember.
That's enough. Or not enough. Trying to get
the old song's lyric straight in my mind,
I recall you tonight. My longing is no less
than on that night when you lifted

your knees & tilted up your hips to take
me in, or give me birth. Nostalgia
is belief drained of religion—you always
wanted me to believe in God, but I couldn't.
Now I can, though not so you'd approve,
who never trusted my ambitions.

YOUTHFUL JOURNALS

They didn't mean much to me in my thirties
& were lost when developers bulldozed
the garage where they were stored in a box
before I could retrieve them, but I wish I had
them now, not that there was much in them
but the despair one feels in one's twenties gazing
at the clear sky over the ocean & hearing
all night the loud thud of breakers as you sleep
beside the first woman who has made her peace
with you. *Taken up with you,* my mother said
with disapproval though she herself had
taken up with a man who would turn out to be
only the ghost of a father—a curtain of rain
off the ocean that drenches the lemon trees
& moves inland to dissolve in the heat of
the valley. In the Bible only the holiest men
are taken up into heaven without dying & that
is the feeling of such sleep near the ocean.
So I imagine the words of those lost journals
burned in a debris fire at a construction site
near the Pacific Ocean fifteen years ago. Lost
as the light that filtered through the dusty
windows of the beach shack where I first knew
(where I was finally calm enough to understand)
another loved me & knew too that I could draw
the world to me in the shape of a sentence.
I remember writing them more than I remember
what I wrote in them; I am no Platonist
& do not believe those thoughts exist somewhere—
I believe they are gone for good & that no
picture of my brain suffused with radioisotopes
could reconstruct a single word. Good. Fine.
I have forgotten everything that was important
about those years except the fact I knew it
once. That's fine with me now. But last night
I dreamed about the parrots who would settle

summer mornings onto the branches of lemon
& loquat & slice the rinds with razor beaks
strong as an old man's toenail. They woke us
& we made love & rose & dressed & went out
into the morning for breakfast of huevos rancheros
not thinking we would ever have to remember
anything—knowing we already knew everything
there was to know. How to eat. How to sleep.
We were classically poor but romantically happy.
When I wrote them I must have believed
in the soul & that no intelligence was artificial.
I must have believed that the world revealed
itself in the sound of music from a car radio
threading itself into the world of the dream
& in the hiss of tires on wet pavement after rain,
a peal of laughter & the sticky smell of flowers
as bright as fireworks breaking up inside the fog
enveloping the city of my birth, named after
a saint or an explorer. I forget which.

NOT KNOWING

after Rumi

I don't know myself but what do you expect?
I can't say
what prayer is but I stare at the night sky
through my window

& ask *In God's name what should I do?*
The old religions
are stupid with masks & dancing & the end
of the world.

(You see after all they have their attractions.)
The new ones
are worse. Their prophets imagine our souls
are plump

summer leaves—not the nervous blue light
& insipid music
of television that fills our suburban streets
& provinces

in which slaughter & politics are confused.
Not to mention
the history of my own sick nation. How am I
to take any of this

seriously? A long time ago I believed in a God
who might burn
down the house in the middle of the night just
to see how those

creatures down there would bear suffering—
I learned a word
for it: *catastrophe* & I used its syllables
in my prayers.

Images of terror flicker across the screen
but I am sitting
right here beside a river listening to rust-
colored water pour

over slabs of granite. Most nights I can sleep
even with moonlight
filling the room & turning my wife's breasts
coolly into stone.

It amazes me to think that this is how we live.
It amazes me to think
at all for my sentences consist of junctures
& pauses—the stutter

of punctuation & the fussy politics of grammar.
Whereas prayer
is a compulsive song whether it splits the throat
or mutters across

the lips & the tongue in patterns as regular
as planetary motion.
I don't know myself but what can you do?

HIS GHOST SINGS BEFORE LEAVING

Goodbye world of the senses goodbye!
Goodbye
& I mean it to gestures & grievances . . .
It is lovely

to watch
categorical imperatives dissolve as if they
were sunsets . . .
In nature all sentences end in ellipses . . .

Believe me
there is nothing but a wisp of will & that
fading to no big deal, no tunnel of light
flaring toward God.

How to sing this?
Like going to work in the morning—
locking the door
behind you & admiring the tulips & light

falling
on rock cress as you go down the steps . . .
Goodbye
to my golf swing & usual hat—to my wife

& the dogs
our quarrels & affections. Goodbye
to books
good & bad & to friends almost as sweet

as the books—
I regret only that I am unable to read—
it's not that death's dark . . . I can admire
the asphodel

but words
on a page are transparent as air . . .
I can remember—just barely, like writing—
the curve

of her back muscled & smooth as flowing
river water
on which sunlight falls & falters. I'm that bird
who hangs in the air,

an idea loose in the world without
thought. A song
that doesn't know what it is . . . Far below
a tune drifts through

the kitchen window the faucet dripping
a crazy signature
sunlight praising each bead of water
splattering in the sink.

SEEING THE LIGHT

At the cross, at the cross
Where I first saw the light . . .

—Old hymn

I promise never to say anything again
about my family or the calamities of spirit
they visited upon me. Today I went
with one of my dogs out into the woods,
where it is fall. The leaves transfused
by late afternoon sunlight performed a glory
no memory of hurt can erase or ruin.

If you can demonstrate that your father's
failure to have loved you as he should is
equal to one photon striking one atom in these
changing leaves I will admit the self is more
important than our prayers. It was religion
they used against me & it has taken me this
long to free my breath in the form of

a prayer. It wasn't much—a short note
of thanks for all this. A *note,* I mean, like music,
though I've never been able to sing.
It may have been the dog taught me with his
short, sharp barks at leaf-rustle & twig-crack.
(With this I invoke Fr. Hopkins, the sad priest
so broken by his yearning & yet so glad.)

THEORY OF THE LYRIC

The difficult art
is not the dream or the song
but adequate notation.

While falling asleep
I say it over & over:
amanuensis.

Amanuensis—
abstract & explicit
the act it implies

is indecent & for that
desirable. At the moment of
highest tension

noun & verb
collapse—the pen dropped.
The sexual arts attend

to what they love without
reserving anything
for the self.

The lyric is dumb—
amanuensis:
singing to ourselves.

BIRCHES ABOVE THE RIVER

I think of these birches as
the beautiful sisters—
They whisper in Greek

stories that predate
the sacred & profane—
sunlight blinds & clarifies

the river & wind
cups its surface revealing
the interior of turbulence.

It is the physical
world that powers your religions.
It is the physical world of powers.

2.

The world has no memory.

—Thomas Hardy, *The Mayor of Casterbridge*

IGNORANCE

My stance is passional toward the universe & you.

—Alice Fulton

I have been ignorant of women.
Stupid about your bodies & worse
about your minds—
I do not

know whether yours are different
in principle
from my own, but my ignorance has been
my bliss

so that your
gestures dancing reveal only now
in my shamed memory their freight
of angers—

even as you were
passional toward me, your understanding
exceeded my own.
For example, women sent into asylums

& convents because they talked too much
or cracked
queer jokes where they may be heard
or simply

cackled at the beauty of the morning
overcome
by the raw sweetness of the air

or who held
opinions counter to the melodies
of history
which is bland & unphilosophical.

Poets hushed by illiteracy.
My own loves, B & C, dear A,
forgive—my ignorance of beauty & my failure

to understand the supple strength
of your arms
& hearts as you embraced me
the most

imperfect
of lovers & my failure to understand
myself even in the clarifying light
of your trust—

I am ashamed as one who
trying to impress drinks too much at dinner
& ends

splattering his shoes
in the parking lot—everyone
looking on.

MAGICAL THINKING

. . . du nombre des amoureux sains

—Villon

"Dick-for-brains," I heard a woman say under her breath, contempt
streaking her voice like staphylococcus. It's true the man walking
away with shoulders pitched forward was graceless—some of us
grow up never learning where to put our hands when talking to a
   woman,
or whether the jacket ought to be buttoned or unbuttoned
& under what circumstances, *ergo cit.*

I honor his high lyric impulse, finding some language to carry
the burden of desire. *Item:* Say we're standing in the sort of place
friends come after work to have a drink. A little soul, not too loud.
The world at a comfortable distance. Nobody dragged her in here
with her contempt for desire. The pleasure named by dirty words
has a sacred place in the world of the imagination.

When I was a bartender closing the place, I'd clunk a quarter
in the jukebox & punch the buttons for "The Girls All Get Prettier
at Closing Time" to mock the crowd of drunks & half-drunks milling
toward the door with six-packs underneath their arms & hope
draining from their bodies. I'm not so insensible now, having learned
the value of even the lowest kinds of lust.

Men (I speak in defense of my gauche brothers)—some fleeing
domestic terrors, some their own dreams, or even memories
of mother & father flinging plates at each other across a sunlit kitchen
Saturday mornings before going off to hump noisily in the bedroom—
will say anything for the chance to bury themselves in the mystery of sex.
It can be worth any lie when deep in the night

the bar is closing & all the therapeutic homilies in the world don't
   add up
to the blue synaptic snap & dazzle of anticipation: a dream in which
decency is suspended without consequences, as in Eden. Prelapsarian:

reptiles nestling in warm mud on a riverbank. *Item:* I am sitting in
   that bar
with my friend when a young woman walks in in a dress that fits her
the way an auxiliary verb slides back & forth

in a balanced sentence—a field of summer flowers, she absorbs
& spills delight without stint. I defy you to deny this which is one part
of the world speaking fluently to other parts. I don't care what you say,
the soul music thrumming from the jukebox is superior to any theory
of the self. Contempt for desire is a sin against nature. Consider
a fact from ethnography: In India

followers of the god Shiva are required to spend a part of their lives
cross-dressing, acting like morons, singing nonsense, gesticulating
lewdly at women—especially this—& farting & trembling while they beg
their food & pray loudly like Christopher Smart in the streets of London
in the eighteenth century who died in the king's prison for debtors,
still opposing Newton & materialism.

Item: "dick-for-brains." Men say it of someone who's fucked up
something it's assumed we're good at—a poker hand, buying a car,
building a shed, punctuating the last sentence of an argument with
physical or intellectual violence. It translates *dumb fuck,* the radical hook
or slice of masculine incompetence. But we admire him, the man
who will do anything for love, even fail.

We hate him, for he engenders disgust with ourselves. For he puts
everything we've earned to the test. He demands we prove ourselves
against the Devil, who is willing to admit he likes crawling into bed
with women & likes thinking about it as much as doing it, though
   he knows,
because he is the Devil, the ontological difference between doing it
& thinking about it. He knows it is here that thinking matters most.

SIX NOTATIONS IN A SPRING JOURNAL

1. Deep Religious Faith
   I watch this evening through the dust-
   streaked motel window as light settles
   over a field & a pair of hawks
   spiral upward on a column
   of warming air. Bare trees absorb
   spring sunlight. I know description
   is only a ritual in the service
   of the empirical dream that
   the available world is all the world
   there is, but it renders raw perception
   understandable—tonight
   on the grainy motel television
   there is a program about raptors.
   Eagles, like spawning salmon
   in hereditary streams, return
   to mate in the same branches
   where they fledged—I watch birds of prey
   sweep through the ideal atmosphere
   of television & almost weep
   from gratitude. What do I know
   about the stark minds of predators?
   Next to nothing. Oh, not even that much.
   Leaving the house this morning,
   I heard a robin sing from the still
   darkness of the vacant lot across
   the street. As I turned onto the main road,
   my headlights flashed across the route signs
   so I thought in passing of talismans
   belonging to the unimportant gods
   who camp beside roads & of those
   gilded crosses carried in processions
   by believers. Every object
   in this light hums with loneliness.

2. Transcendentalism
    In Los Angeles we walked the beach,
    shy with each other though married
    a year. An offshore wind blew breakers
    into sheets of silver spray that broke
    the sun into its spectral colors.
    Making love in our once-elegant
    hotel room near the ocean, we felt
    like strangers, though our undressed
    bodies could get along without us.
    The body is a world I understand.
    The rumpled polyester blankets
    glowed when evening light off the Pacific
    poured into the room, dry air making
    the artificial fabric spark.

3. Determinism
    Another friend with cancer.
    Its white ropes braid her spine like ivy
    that kills the tree it clings to . . .
    I slammed around all morning
    angry, inarticulate, angry. At lunch
    a friend branded me with moral
    inconsistency in one of those
    vague arguments intellectuals
    engage in like digestion. I stared
    straight ahead, then went home to dig
    furiously in the garden, the swirling
    wind that comes in cold behind
    a front tearing leaves from the maple,
    the dog sheltering under the hedge
    & the irritating whistle
    of the wind around the corners
    of the house like a dream that sticks
    all day, *making itself felt.*
    I remember my father standing
    stiffly at my mother's grave, light
    swirling in the poplar trees above

the funeral & the idiot
hired for his comforting words
galling the air with pious bilge.
Language folds back on itself, a clever
origami bird that cannot fly.
So, light on those tall weeds out there—
is that the whole picture? Behind
the trees, there must be more, a big lake
rough with wind & acid light.

4. Angel in the Kitchen
    Stopping part way home to see friends
    in the Midwest, I find myself talking
    to people I hardly know. Drinks all round.
    Politics & literature. I watch
    a young woman lean backward
    in her chair, eyes fixed for balance
    on some invisible horizon &
    I am grateful for this luxury—
    the momentary silence in the kitchen.
    I wonder how anyone will speak.
    The body keeps us in the universe
    of things. Her wrists curled through the back
    of her chair, she grasps its spokes, holding
    her arms behind her like wings. I know
    that the long muscles of the arm
    & the silken ones that lace the eyelid
    don't always tell the truth, that the body
    conceives lies as easily as the mind. I know.

5. Particle or Wave
    Most of us in this tidy suburban
    airport would just as soon have *arrived*
    by now as be here where we are,
    in transit. These tired men my father's age
    slumped in chairs beneath flickering
    monitors listing departures
    & arrivals surely wish their hands

were right now gripping the hands of
their associates, content with the
familiar greetings, looking forward
to seeing kids & wives tomorrow night.
Not all of us are tired of travel.
Some—children, young soldiers, families
going on their first airplane & edgy
go-getters with beat-up briefcases
& inexpensive suits—are enthralled
by all of this: smell of floor wax,
backlit real estate listings, screens
flashing ads, a version of weather
& quizzes designed to test our
factual knowledge of the world,
glossy menus in the coffee shop,
a red Buick parked on carpet remnants
in the lobby, a gift shop filled
with bright artifacts—proof you went
away, & then came back.
From the lounge I watch a guard as she
X-rays carry-on belongings:
books turned into ghosts, coat hangers
into the bones of small animals
called shirts & the folded suits
of business travelers, almost invisible,
into abstract drawings of desire.
Everything, reduced to this
empirical glimmer, looks sinister.

6. Grammar

Home this evening, I sit beneath
a Xerox copy of a photograph—
a *lekythos*—a vase thrown & decorated
for a burial in Athens
two thousand years ago. Painted
on it is the figure of a muse pointing
at a small bird near her bare feet,
her gesture indicative, perfectly

grammatical. It seems we've always
wanted to sing, despite the difficulty
of balancing the phrase & the particles
that link our clauses awkwardly
to things. Earlier, out with the dog,
I heard another robin sing—perched,
it turned out, on the receiving strut
at the center of a microwave dish,
which amplified the pure, clear tones
of his singing—if you want to call it
singing—that has no function but to
place him in the world. Cock Robin pays
a price—nerve, blood & sperm saturated
with the millimeter waves
transmitting the steady beat
of human talk, jangling that other
language coded in his chromosomes—
syntax of survival, truth
in the biological sense. Song makes
a poor accommodation with
the shimmering world of things I love.
Why would I ever want to give it up?

WILDLIFE OF THE DESERT

Saints expected a dead place, but there is life
in the desert, all wild. Hermits who thought

to get away from everything but their own minds
found scorpions & black widows, the moon

casting devastating light into their shacks.
Centipedes folding themselves into blankets.

The alert melodic whistles of owls & the silence
of their momentum snatching an incautious mouse.

All night the coyotes yip & sneak nimbly down
from the red rocks where they hunt to the dumps

to lick out the insides of cans that will rust
for generations before becoming an oxide stain

on the caustic sand undisturbed by rain. Glass
is eternal, let it stand for the soul, turning blue

under the impact of light. If you walk here
walk with stick in hand to ward off the diamondback

& sidewinder. Thirst simplifies desire,
catches the hermit dreaming of water & women

holding up their breasts to be kissed, or building
his own city in this place—the devil

winning his bet—filled with what he fled.
The desert, for all its clarity, is no more pure

than the soul, which buzzes with contradiction,
a splintered fragment of amethyst, this—

SONG

A stalk of evening primrose
in the ditch—
a strip of silver light across the green
surface of the pond.

The yellow
flowers strike the air with light
& the air
is still, the water an unbroken face.

Oh please shut up he thinks
the neighbors arguing again.
He will wake
past midnight—the single note

of a restless
bird—a byte of punctuation that
translated means
I do not understand. Say again.

THEORY OF TRAGEDY

How can we believe in anything again?

—Echecrates, in *The Phaedo*

Why didn't the first philosopher want to go on living
among the sun-warmed stones of his native city?
Wasn't the music, microtonal as sunlight on paving stones,
worthy of him? Didn't he have friends
whose particular talk he loved more than the cool beauty
of ideas? There was as yet no definition of tragedy.

His students say the old man believed deeply
in the clarifying power of disputation, urging them
that argument leads always toward truth, though
it never arrives there. He loved to form definitions, believing
them like music, for which, apparently, he had no ear.
There was as yet no definition of tragedy,

though everyone knew what he or she meant by the word—
a certain feeling in the bowel
as you filed from the theater after something by Sophocles,
a bristling of hairs on the small of the neck, evidence
of poison working out toward the skin,
the body politic purging itself of doubt, bending

its confident demotic beneath the weight of music
and dance. But out in the streets Socrates heard the passion
of speech slide into Rhetoric, which was invented, some say,
in order to contain the passions roused
in the populace by the music of speech.
There was, as yet, no definition of tragedy.

Was Socrates so sold on himself he couldn't *imagine*
(the whisper of god in his hairy old ear)
the fine words of those citizens talking among themselves
on the marble steps of the king Archon's palace?

He thought they were dangerous, tugged this way and that
like a tide destroying the walls of the city.

The rationalist philosopher Sherlock Holmes loved
to play music when not testing blood
stains on a carpet—scratching away like crazy at his violin—
a fine old instrument better than his skill—making music
the more terrible for its awful Victorian sentiment.
The problem of tragedy is how close it always must come

to sentiment. Both these philosophers hated democracy—
the dirty feet of the mob, the bumbling stupidity
of the man in the street, who loves the fat that sticks to his own bones
and therefore is no fit audience for tragedy. Tonight
as I read, the faint odor of skunk drifts through the window.
I imagine the dogs of Athens raising their noses

into an ancient breeze off the Aegean carrying the sour smell
of the philosopher's corpse after he has accepted poison
from the jury of citizens. Would the private eye, so adept
at uncovering what others called *tragedy,* have been able to determine
the cause of death by examining the famous scene in the prison?
And had the first detective sniffed out the hemlock,

would he have deduced the fibers of the soul floating loose
in the damp air of the cell? What would he have thought
of the crooked smile on the round gray face?
And what analysis could have made the tears smearing the faces
of those wealthy and self-sufficient men gathered there
in the prison yield useful knowledge?

The outer stones of the prison, already warmed
by morning sun, and the city's air vibrant with music rising
from its streets, the shopkeepers sold fish, copper, fresh bread,
and the red figure ware common to that place and time, often
depicting Clytemnestra's bloody betrayal of Agamemnon
or famous episodes in Odysseus' long journey back

to his wife—both impossible fictions! The dogs might have
made some music with those old bones, even lacking
a theory of tragedy, which is really a theory of knowledge.
Tonight, odor of skunk hanging like a philosopher's soul
in the air, I sit beneath a Xerox copy of a photograph—one of those
Greek vases called a *lekythos,* this one showing a daughter of Memory,

loosely draped, feet bare, sexy, her right hand indicating
a songbird on a branch sketched near her feet.
Without a definition of tragedy, we cannot understand
the dance our words and grammar pattern intersecting
the facts of the palpable world—a maple tree's black
branches against the amber/blue stripes of sunset,

perfume of skunk and wood smoke hanging in the air.
The old man always said his wisdom was nothing but ignorance,
and at the end of his life he couldn't prove the soul
survives the body. Perhaps it was nothing but a feeling,
like tragedy, which is only the awkward singing
of a small bird on a flimsy branch pointing toward memory.

PORNOGRAPHY

Combien qu'il soit rudement fait
La matiere est si tres notable
Qu'elle amende tout le mesfait.

—Villon

The body is the instrument on which imagination plays.
The temple prostitute sent by the king to seduce & civilize
Enkidu brought her guitar along, as well as her makeup kit.
She sang him away from the animals & taught him language
by whispering songs into his sunburned ears that rang
with sympathetic chords. Thus he forgot his nature & world.

Ask King Gilgamesh—the truest friend is the wild man who
has just begun to master the vocabularies of the city
& still dreams the live & flickering savanna hot with sun, blood
staining the grass where a lion has killed a zebra, flies. Peace.
Resting in the shade as the sun passes the ferocious zenith.
His memories give him strength the king can bend to use.

Well-practiced, she took his hand & smoothed it with her own.
The city flourishes upon sophisticated grammars, but sometimes
a gesture goes so deep we feel it like a breath, or song
that drifts from a smoky alley recalling low hills flickering
under sun, blood. Or late at night two people without reason flare
matchlight into each other's eyes & reach out their hands toward . . .

Impossible now to recover that which once they were
before the gesture. The body live with animal faith is the instrument
on which imagination plays. Someone lowers the radio to a whisper
& flicks on the lobby television in an SRO hotel. The old men
scratch their beards & settle on a greasy couch, blowing smoke.
Two fighters are entering the ring, white beneath the klieg lights;

on-screen colors flicker in & out of register revealing the three souls
of each man—vegetal, animal & rational. The referee dances
across the ring, a ghostly figure in charge of making beauty out

of violence. Next door, the movies are threaded into the projectors
at the Apple Theater, an old garage perched above an on-ramp where
the grungy carpets & scarlet velvet curtains muffle the footsteps

of the patrons, but not the sanctified shrieks of the actresses who
fuck the audience with light. The beefy lips of their vaginas are swollen
as the gash above one fighter's eye, who is peering through a mist
of blood for his opponent's face, an image of the truth collecting
on the cerebral cortex at the back of his shaken brain. The king
smashes his fist like a hammer into the jaw of the wild man

from the steppe, who does not crumble but strikes a ferocious blow
to the king's belly that makes him shit blood on the ground.
Cracking the curbs, they fight forty days & nights outside the tavern
where posters advertise LIVE NUDE GIRLS nipples & pubic hair
obliterated by a cold black bar. They fall into each other's arms.
Thus is born the psyche of Western Man—a brawl outside a bar

at the beginning of history. From this beginning, a short step
leads to fear of death & terror in the face of women. In the movies
they are slugging it out to an endless loop of bass guitar.
The rhetoric of literature since the ancients admits sexual desire
as well as its twin politics: Aphrodite & Ares strung up in Hephestos'
cunning net—Homer's dirty joke in the form of an aside

after the women (every one a queen or princess) have gone to bed
& only the slave girls dark & sinuous as the Nile & half naked
in the heat are still up dozing in the shadowed corners of the room—
their imperishable desire a melody that persists through history,
modal & efficient, turning up under different titles. Aficionados
watch to see if the champion has broken a sweat by the time

he enters the ring. Sweat equals desire & readiness, salt & sweet.
There are pheromones to perpetuate the species & others designed
specifically by the gods to break your heart. Didn't you know?
The old gods live in the chaotic interstices of natural selection, ever
& anon creating the world. That's *his* territory, the culture hero
Dick-for-Brains. Usually portrayed iconographically as a *roué,*

the noun derived from the past participle of the old French word
for *breaking on the wheel*. A sport, a wolf (in outdated jive), some
poor doofus who, having failed again, is driving that stretch of highway
between 2:00 A.M. & dawn angry as hell & all its angels who will
again be falling drunk & disappointed into bed because he is a man
who deserves his fate, unable in every account to turn irony

upon experience. Not one of the heroes, he will do anything
for love. The old men are disappointed because the fighters have
battered each other to a draw. No money changes hands. They
can hear the crunch of gravel as the patrons next door pull out
of the parking lot & glide around the corner, their tail lights
smeared like blood on the pavement wet with increasing rain.

SEEING STARS: THE NEW COSMOLOGY

That was
the winter a pulse of gamma radiation—an *explosion*
(the word
is beggared by fact:

an event
next only in release of energy to that originary
apocalypse
that brought this local universe streaming out

of the vacuum)—
washed over our horizon, a flash flood following
a cloudburst.
I look into that region

of sky picked out as
Ursa Major or Big Dipper & see the place where
space tore open,
but all I can imagine is a black flower of light—

not mystical
but as empirical as the weeds in the ditch along
the road
which I know are there though I cannot see them

in the dark:
joe-pye weed, evening primrose, vetch, bracken,
smoke bush,
yellow flag, bristle-grass, goldenrod, knotweed,

chickweed, duckweed, milkweed, white clover
like the stars
& red clover like the stars & asters named for stars
& mullein

the odd biannual with fuzzy leaves & tall spikes
like yellow flames—
this is their year for the explosion of their flowers:
next year

they will put out only a tuft of leaves low to the ground
gathering strength
from the rain.
& nightshade that can poison livestock & children attracted

to its bright berries hard as the nipples of the virgins who
once used
its decoction to enhance the beauty of their eyes
by enlarging

the pupils.
It made them appear receptive to the gazes of suitors,
a beauty
that made the world indistinct—the enlarged aperture

reducing the depth of field registered by their pretty eyes.
I am such a suitor
after beauty gazing into the night sky & recognizing this . . .
gesture—a wave

of farewell
as innocent as Adam's as he watched them walk away,
the animals,
after he had named them & knew what they were.

MAGICAL THINKING: WHAT COUNTS AS EVIDENCE

To think, not to dream, that is our duty.

—Van Gogh

When the police
& prosecutors couldn't
find any evidence
that the man they had
in custody for the crime
of raping & murdering
the little girl had been
where they said or done
what they claimed, they
put down in their notes
that he had told them
a dream with details
"only the killer could know"
& thus moved into
the realm of the biblical.
Where did the meaning
of Pharaoh's dreams reside
when he told them
to his servant Joseph?
In whose mind?

They were making
a claim about knowledge
& were thus *philosophers*
though later accounts
call into question
the specific relation
between their sworn
sentences & what we are
pleased to call the facts
of the case & whose existence—
however contingent—
is presumed to be a quality

of the world external
to the policemen's selves.
They were bad philosophers
even if they were good
storytellers. That is where
language enters the picture.
They had a story they
liked & were reluctant
to give up. & so they
said it was a dream
which is the kind of story
no one can argue with
because dreams come
to us—we do not call them,
which is what gives
them their power
to enlighten & confuse
the facts, by which we mean
those things that lie outside
our selves. Those
important things insisting
we are not dreaming
but awake here, now.

SEEING STARS: A BALLAD OF EMPIRICISM

That was
the winter the truck's heater quit
& we had
no money—those clear mornings

the air too cold
to hold moisture stars of ice formed
on the inside
of the windshield. Driving to work

I looked through hazy galaxies
of frost
a blue-collar god in his beat-up
blue truck—

That's how I felt when everything
went wrong.
Impervious. That was the winter
the axe blade

shattered
striking a frozen chunk of maple
& that
was the winter the water heater blew

spraying
candescent blue sparks & steam across
the basement.
That was the winter the wide world

of physical
objects insisted they be noticed
categorically
in our lives. That was the winter

the crisis
in our cold hearts wrote itself large
on the face
of things. Backing out of the driveway

the truck's
tires marked curving Xs in the snow:
first elements
in an alphabet with no grammar

& little syntax.
Behind me this morning as I pull onto
the county road
dry snow rises in clouds so complex

only an equation
requiring all the time remaining in
the world
to solve could describe their vortices

& pools of light. That was the winter
I decided
I could bear my life as long as God
would just keep away from me.

ABANDONED BLUETICK BITCH

Numbed with self-loathing,
we abandon the emissaries
of grace. Chained to a tree

beside the empty rental
she hollowed out a den
for herself & her young.

By the time we found her
the water they'd left her
was a couple of days gone.

When the water was gone
she would have slept, not dreaming,
letting the pups nurse

her sparse milk & when
the smallest died she ate it to keep
her strength & cleanse the den,

depriving coy dogs & foxes
an expedient scent.
It's likely there were two more

before we found her.
Ribs covered by a tissue of dry skin,
she was nothing—a shadow

on the dirt & was just able
to raise her head & take
a little water from my hand

before turning to nose
her three live pups awake.
Reader, it is true, there is

horror everywhere worse
than this & cruelty that beggars
imagination, but this

is local & particular; these were
my neighbors did this,
who, without even the excuse

of psychosis, committed this wrong.
Who live in this same light
& shadow I live in.

Let us kill one another
with heedless abandon—we deserve it—
but not these poor relations

whose lives are without malice
& whose motives are transparent.
Let us kill one another.

SUPERSTITION

Walk forty-seven mile of barbwire,
Use a cobra snake for a necktie,
I got a brand new house on the roadside
Made from rattlesnake hide.
I got a brand new chimney made on top
Made out of a human skull . . .
Now come on take a little walk with me,
Now tell me, Who do you love?
Who do you love? Who do you love?

—Bo Diddley

> At noon the upright human body casts
>   no shadow,
> or the shadow is driven straight down
>   into the body.
> Sharp grass blades & fat stones disappear
>   in glare.
> The road shimmers & puddles with black
>   light in the distance.
> The Romans believed ghosts struck at noon,
>   explosions
> of white-hot sunlight flaring out from
>   the base of a wall,
> a white column flayed in light. Disaster
>   always
> takes place outside the hot, slow pulse
>   of the world,
> and boredom, which casts no shadow, uncoils
>   at midday,
> among the tumbling demons of light, so
>   they believed.
> Jesus must have found the man who lived
>   among the tombs
> trembling & naked at noon, bleeding
>   and chained,

cowering in the brilliant Mediterranean
    air. & when
he cast them out with a white stare, the devils
    screwed themselves
into the swaying bellies of nearby swine,
    who pitched
into the sea. & when a sane man staggered
    into town that
afternoon, only the old men remembered him.
    In the dead air
of these suburbs, sunlight is smashing
    the sidewalk slowly
to grit, making the blurry music of noon
    that no one
wants to hear. The fretting baby quiets,
    seeming to hold
her breath so long her mother hurries
    to the crib
to see what is the matter. A young man
    with the flat stare
and autistic sneer of criminal authority
    pauses, robbing a store
by the highway, to lift a quart of beer
    from the cooler—
rolling the cool bottle over his forehead,
    he notices
the spastic flies trapped behind the plastic
    beer sign,
where, also, a little blood is spattered
    like punctuation.
The girl waiting in the car will be glad,
    he thinks,
for his thoughtfulness. He checks
    his reflection
in the glass door going out, waves back
    his hair
with his hand, a gesture a little like
    a salute.

A compressor hums out back—one low note—
    and ghosts
flicker in the dust kicked up by trucks.
    At noon
the maenads tore young Pentheus apart,
    says Euripides—
during the stalled momentum & sexual
    panic of midday. Later,
as rain dripped quietly into the cistern,
    they were very sorry.
For an instant the young housewife is glad
    her child is dead,
and she dreams—the windows burning at noon—
    of passionate travel
to romantic islands. The baby coughs
    and squalls
in the heat & she lifts it from the crib,
    smoothing
its damp hair & cooing her gratitude—
    she will be able
to keep thinking of herself as herself.
    Tiresias, in wide hat,
strolls the sidewalk & scowls at the
    cool windows
of the houses. A husband coming home
    passes his wife's
lover coming toward him in traffic, singing
    with the radio.
Who do you love? Who do you love?
    The song rough
with static. A detective is collecting
    evidence:
the store's air conditioning is on—
    heat flows
from the clerk's cheek into the cold
    linoleum,
doing no useful work—one more example
    of general

disorder, molecules smashed to weightless
      subatomic
particles in the center of the sun
      and streaming
through what we think of as the substance
      of the earth.

3.

Biết làm sao! Chúng ta quá nhiều lời.

Ở những chỗ ra cần nói ngắn.

What can be done! We've spoken too many words.

We needed only a few.

—Bằng Việt, "Khoảng Cách Giữa Lời"

EIGHTEENTH-CENTURY VIETNAMESE BUDDHA

His head is bald
& the lines in his forehead
repeat the folds of skin

where his modest belly
tucks beneath his ribs.
The Buddha is smiling

& contemplating, one is certain,
the cosmological constant
& the value of Omega,

which contains the directions
for assembling the universe
& for tearing it down

like a tent after the circus.
One arm is raised—parting
the gilt folds of his gown—

in a gesture that suggests
he is about to reveal
the precise secrets of science

by which we will discover
our human part
in the wave of probability

that is the world.
But it is an artist's trick—
the smiling man knows nothing.

He counts like the rest of us
on his fingers & toes,
& though he has looked

at the night sky with some attention,
it wasn't long before he went in
& took some wine

by the brazier & thought
with no little weariness
of his students who would arrive

at first light. He decided
to instruct them on the difference
between day & night.

That is why the artist
portrayed him laughing
as if at his own good joke—

The artist, too, has students
who demand to know
the secrets of the world—

as if he could pull them
from his pocket
with his carving tools,

his paints & brushes,
his gold leaf & his burnisher.
As if he knew anything.

THUA ÔNG*

*Out of the horror there rises
a musical ache that is beautiful.*

—James Wright

An anger so quiet it becomes music—
    a gesture
like music—word without alphabet;
a gesture that breaks toward God;
    a single
moment without confusion. This is

    how to turn
philosophy to use . . . I have no idea
    how the monk's

mind worked as he was driven down
    from Hue
to Saigon in a blue & white Peugeot—

    (parked now
in a garage back in Hue it still runs
    a little rust

    like blood
on the fender, a few gallons in the tank).
    I don't know

what to think. *It is as if,* Quang Duc,
    you might
still have to go there again, saying

    prayers
characteristic of your sect to prepare
    your body

*"Thưa Ông" means "Greetings, elder uncle," in Vietnamese.

for fire.
I have peered a long time at the photo's
    grainy smoke—

it shows you surrounded by brilliance.
    Behind you
the mundane little car & insubstantial

through heat-haze your friends standing
    hands clasped
apparently in prayer. They said only

your heart remained but that must
    be only a story.
Corrupt & sexually cold, Madam Nhu

    referred to you
as "barbecue" & offered fuel & matches
    to others who

might wish to follow your example
    her contempt
streaked with the infections of her fear.

Sir, I don't know what to think—what
    certainty
flicked the lighter sending you to heaven?

    (If history
can be thought of as a kind of heaven.)
    Freed from history

by entering
into it I don't think you meant to say
    anything—

the clarity of your gesture a prayer
    acknowledging
a silence in the heart of noise. *Amen.*

THE FALL OF SAIGON

"Light, Fresh, Exotic & Delicious!" reads
the big print
in a restaurant advertisement in *Viet Nam News*
the English paper

in HCMC where
the war-broken haul themselves along on crutches
& in wheeled
contrivances, the heels of their hands dark

calluses glittering
with the quartz of the sidewalk outside the
famous hotel
the unexpected ends of their limbs pink as neon.

They want to show you color pictures of their
families
& how can I deny them this privilege who
might as well

have packed the ordnance into the Phantoms
& Stratofortresses
from 1965 to 1972 for all the good my childish
protest did?

The waitress jokes she wants to marry me
& move
to California & who can blame her? A joke
but offered

with the faintest
eye-flicker of hope. When she gets off work
past midnight
she walks the thirty blocks home & watches

Asian MTV with her brothers & sisters—
& so her head
is full of the same misinformation about love
& money

mine is—we are both incurable romantics.
I would
too—marry her, for she has enchanted me
with music:

between courses she has taken her place
across the room
& played melodies on the den bao that feel
as natural

as water or air & as incomprehensible.
She wasn't born . . .
Even if in a dream we married & learned
each other's

languages we would never understand
each other's
forms of life. She wants me to write & I put
her meticulous

address in my wallet—A year later unfold it
& read its script
like music proving anything can be a song.

TALKING TO GHOSTS

I am sorry you did not live to see
the century dissolve
& the work of language we are pleased to call
the millennium *fssst* out

like a cigarette tipped into a beer bottle, or a star.
You didn't mean
to be a teacher, but you got the job & we hardly
understood you.

You knew Blake & understood his systems
not like a scholar
with an armload of dictionaries—though you loved
dictionaries—

but as a believer, which is to say an apostate
for you had your own
elaborate system of belief in language—the boat
we fill with provisions

& in which we set ourselves adrift. The map is not
the territory
though the map itself can be an object of desire.

We talked one afternoon
about the war—Westmoreland had razed a village
named Ben Suc that morning
(while we had been listening to music)

tucked in a bend
of the Saigon River & it was you who noted
for my benefit
that the Vietnamese word for river is *song;* such

correspondences
don't mean a thing, we know—& I learned this year
it is pronounced
more like *psalm*. You would have loved that fact

as a minute particular.
What infuriated you was the inept use of metaphor
recorded in the papers.
I won't repeat the stupid phrases in your poem . . .

It is a country where people talk to ghosts & for that
reason has less fear
of history than we have here where we are anxious
to keep what we have.

A recent map suggests people have returned to the village
of Ben Suc there
in the bend of the river despite the best efforts of
our language to end it.

AFTERNOON: RADIO NOISE

Early summer: the long light of late afternoon breaks
across the fields—sparrows (who can sing) & starlings
(who can be taught to say words) dart across the live space
of the simmering road before me, each bird searing
a specific virtuoso motion on the air—long cursive
lines before my eyes as I drive into the setting sun, which

ignites the dust & pollen stuck to the truck's cracked windshield:
action at a distance. I will never pass inspection.
A cattle pond in the field to the west burns—a foil
of sunlight—& the afternoon explodes across my field of vision,
relentless as prophecy, in which ordinary verbs break
under the pressure of light, separating into their constituent

particles whose properties must be described in terms of strangeness
& spin. The birds' bodies sing like shrapnel—static fuzzes
the truck's radio—sunspots or the local cops: the atmosphere
filled with blistering voices that ask me to imagine
boy soldiers in [obscured by static] *The invention of lightweight arms
makes children good soldiers.* "There is always a colonel to put

a rifle into the hands of a twelve-year-old," a diplomat remarks
in the capital, his voice dry as salt. The soul of simplicity,
an AK-47 costs six dollars & can be field-stripped
& reassembled by a child of ten. The boys talk into
the microphone, voices disembodied & abstract as buzzing
flies round the eyes & anus of a corpse. This is a form of knowledge

with no music in it & it is criminal to invent lyrical dogs
to snuffle the blood of civil wars. God's voice
from the whirlwind does not believe in History, only in power
& the shifting & terrifying opportunities of myth that
emerge when the mind breaks open with grief. Oedipus
addresses the people of Thebes, taking responsibility for

the broken world sweltering in the heat of late afternoon.
Outside the walls his sons are gathering for war—a boy's voice
reports he joined the army when his mother & father were killed
he can't remember by which side; he cannot name the parts
of his weapon but he has been taught how to fire it;
he has killed some men this morning who were creeping

through the grass at the edge of the camp. The effects of sunlight
in a low latitude—witless & without ironic dimension,
stupidly gorgeous (This poem is stupid with hatred.)
& like music it doesn't say anything. It is the same as sunlight
in equatorial regions. There is some grace in sight though
I know that even looking at things the mind is prickly

with ideas, vision murderous. (Every crackpot ideologue
& revolutionary leader, every colonial overseer with a switch
in his hand has had a gleaming vision of the future & believes
unwaveringly in himself.) *Item:* I retract whatever earlier testament
I may have offered—There is no grace in sunlight. There is no
comfort in the light of things nothing like music. The body

is invisible lying in the grass until the muffled explosion of flies
disturbed by the tramping of soldiers' feet rises from it.
Polynices' eyes have been drained by ants & his opened gut
glistens with maggots. There are only hunger & power
& the power of hunger & hunger for power; there is the king
being led away amid the incessant humming of flies; there is

alternating noise & silence. The dogs tremble with fear at this
army of slim ghosts bearing small arms employing deadly force
with perfect innocence. The body is invisible lying in the grass.
The mind is prickly with ideas, vision murderous. The problem
of tragedy is [shouting obscured by static] to sentiment.
The long light of late afternoon breaks across the fields.

THE DOG IN DAUMIER'S *THE REFUGEES*

Phanopoeia: Throwing the object (fixed or moving)
on to the visual imagination.

—Ezra Pound

> The dog is nothing but a shadow
> on the margin
> of the file of fleeing refugees in Daumier's
> grim picture.
>
> The men came
> in the night / they came in the day.
> They hacked up
> her children into parts—limbs & heads—
>
> with the long knives everywhere known
> as *machetes*—
> used for harvest & murder—
> jumbled
>
> the pieces among the broken furniture—
> the long knives
> bequeathed by conquerors having learned
> home truths.
>
> (You have heard
> this before but how do you construct
> the right verb
> for such actions?) *Before her eyes*—
>
> the phrase
> a seed as hard as the point of a nail—
> a cliché
> that collapses night & day. A knife.

How construe a syntax broken like
these chairs
in the photograph & the bones burned
down into

a gray mud
seeded with broken teeth & impressed
by footprints
of vermin? *Before her eyes.*

So was she murdered—clubbed to her
knees & hacked
fell—legs arms forehead ears breasts
disfigured

but came back to life.
Stands in the sweltering court to tell
what was done.
Left for dead, she says & goes on

in the absolute tense of silence
her story
a transcript without commas but with
a grammar

as rigorous as fire.
Some music is not divided into measures.
*The bodies
of my children were piled on top of me.*

Like the dog in Daumier's grim painting
she has an interest
in the human world but is detached from it
seeing through

the gray gauze
of her grief, each word a bucket of water
she must haul
up from the well into daylight to drink.

I wasn't there.
I have no direct knowledge, only this
phanopoeia.
I heard her say she crawled away

from her house
& lay still in the weeds surrounded by
the distinctive
odor of corpses baking in the sun.

Imagine
the killers / your neighbors fanning out
through the village
& imagine the equatorial sunlight that

falls straight down
so no blade of grass casts a shadow.
The dog
her children had cared for came to her

in the field
where she lay & licked the maggots from
her wounds
saving her from the death intended for her.

The dog drawn by its own need returned
to the woman
with hands too broken to dig
for the potatoes

where she lay in the field & who dug
with her teeth
until the dog came & pawed the dirt
so she could eat.

This is the man
she says looking at the figure in blue shirt
& shorts.
He appears very far away, a vanishing

point
at the far end of an unpopulated vista.
He stands in the universal posture
of prisoners

a man without a story because he was so
easily buggered
by the gaudy stories of others.
A man whose silence is different from

the silence
of the murdered & different from that of
the dogs
who have fallen silent all through that country.

SIX SEEDS

Đi Đấu Dấy?

1.

When they meet each other
on the street people here
ask, "Where you going?"
I walk through the city
on a cool day in fall
everyone watching me
wanting to know where
I'm going & so quickly.

2.

In a dream last night
a ragged little boy held
out six pumpkin seeds to me
in his grimy right hand
but I refused them.
This morning the question is
what would have grown
had I accepted the gift.

3.

Rilke says the poet
the human being must
look hard at the body
in the ditch, but this morning
I turned away from the man
cutting a duck's neck
in the alley & draining
the blood into a basin.

4.

Rain splatters down
amidst the motorbikes
& I think of the word for rain—
mưa. It is riding through
traffic that I practice
the language, reading signs.
Seeing the swerving dance
of lights—

5.

one fabric with a pattern
spread too wide to see
or pieces broken from
an urn & scattered in my alley?
Each shop is a universe
with branching trees of logic.
Each conversation demands
I fall in love again with

6.

what I mean. An old story
says a prince exiled
to an island planted seeds
dropped by birds & grew
rich selling the melons
to passing ships. Impressed,
his father the king
brought him home for his story.

FOR WITTGENSTEIN

Days are like grass the wind moves over:
first the wind & then the silence—
what cannot be said we must pass over
in silence, or play some music over
in our heads. Silently, a wind goes over
(we know from the motion of the grass).
Days are like grass; the wind goes over:
first the wind & then the silence.

NOTES

Most of the epigraphs are self-explanatory and are credited where they occur. The epigraph for "Pornography," however, may require translation. In Galway Kinnell's version it reads: "Although the style may be crude / The matter itself is so potent / It makes up for the defects." The epigraph for "Magical Thinking," also from Villon, is " . . . numbered among the saints of love."

Ngô Đình Diệm was the president of the South Vietnamese regime from 1954 until his assassination in 1963.

The epigraph at the head of section 3 is from the Vietnamese poet Bằng Việt's poem "Khoảng Cách Giữa Lời" ["The Space between Words"]. The text of the entire poem, in a translation by Nguyễn Ba Chung and Kevin Bowen, can be found in *Mountain River: Vietnamese Poetry of the Wars, 1948–1993* (University of Massachusetts Press, 1998).

Although intentionally generalized, the situations and quotations in "Afternoon: Radio Noise" and "The Dog in Daumier's *The Refugees*" are drawn from radio reports of the civil war in Mozambique and the genocide in Rwanda.

THE OHIO STATE UNIVERSITY PRESS / *THE JOURNAL*

AWARD IN POETRY   David Citino, Poetry Editor

2000	Lia Purpura	*Stone Sky Lifting*
1999	Mary Ann Samyn	*Captivity Narrative*
1998	Walt McDonald	*Blessings the Body Gave*
1997	Judith Hall	*Anatomy, Errata*
1996	John Haag	*Stones Don't Float: Poems Selected and New*
1995	Fatima Lim-Wilson	*Crossing the Snow Bridge*
1994	David Young	*Night Thoughts and Henry Vaughan*
1993	Bruce Beasley	*The Creation*
1992	Dionisio D. Martínez	*History as a Second Language*
1991	Teresa Cader	*Guests*
1990	Mary Cross	*Rooms, Which Were People*
1989	Albert Goldbarth	*Popular Culture*
1988	Sue Owen	*The Book of Winter*
1987	Robert Cording	*Life-list*

THE GEORGE ELLISTON POETRY PRIZE

1987	Walter McDonald	*The Flying Dutchman*
1986	David Weiss	*The Fourth Part of the World*
1985	David Bergman	*Cracking the Code*